World Book's Learning Ladders

Good Food for You

WORLD BOOK

a Scott Fetzer company
Chicago
www.worldbook.com

233 N. Michigan Avenue
Chicago, IL 60601
U.S.A.

For information about other World Book publications, visit our website at
http://www.worldbook.com or call **1-800-WORLDBK (967-5325).**

For information about sales to schools and libraries, call **1-800-975-3250 (United States); 1-800-837-5365 (Canada).**

Library of Congress Cataloging-in-Publication Data

Good food for you.
p. cm. -- (World Book's learning ladders)
Summary: "Introduction to nutrition and healthy eating using simple text, illustrations, and photos. Features include puzzles and games, fun facts, a resource list, and an index"-- Provided by publisher.
Includes index.
ISBN 978-0-7166-7739-0
1. Nutrition--Juvenile literature. 2. Food--Juvenile literature. I. World Book, Inc.
QP141.G624 2011
612.3--dc22

2010027031

This edition:
ISBN: 978-0-7166-7838-0 (print)
Set 2 ISBN: 978-0-7166-7845-8 (print)

E-book editions:
ISBN: 978-0-7166-4121-6 (EPUB3)
ISBN 978-0-7166-2514-8 (PDF)

Printed in China by Shenzhen Wing King Tong
Paper Products Co., Ltd.
Shenzhen, Guangdong
3rd printing May 2014

Photographic credits: Cover: © Liza McCorkle, iStockphoto; WORLD BOOK illustration by Q2A Media; Shutterstock; p4, p20: Getty Images; p6, p8, p23: Alamy Images; p10, p11, p14, p15, p18, p19, p26, p27, p28, p30: Shutterstock; p16: Landov

Illustrators: WORLD BOOK illustration by Q2A Media; WORLD BOOK illustration by Richard Bonson, The Art Agency

What's inside?

This book tells you about the different food groups. It is important to eat from the five food groups every day.

Food groups

Every day, people should eat foods from each of the five food groups. The five food groups are grains, vegetables, fruits, milk, and meat and beans. Eating from the five food groups helps to give your body the nutrients (nourishing things) it needs.

Some people are vegetarians. They do not eat meat. They may not eat milk products, either. Many people are vegetarian for health or religious reasons.

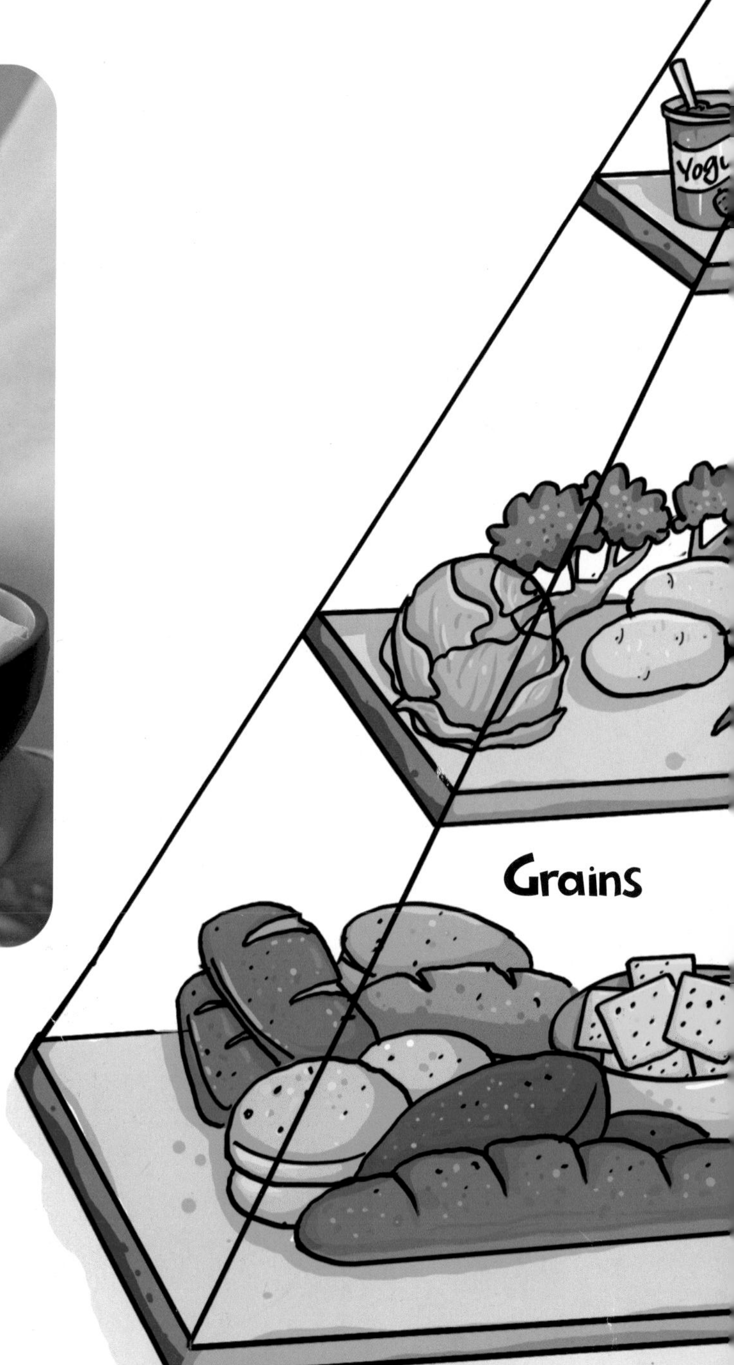

Fats are not a food group. But we need a small amount of fat each day.
CHIPS
Candy
Mayonnaise
Milk
MILK
MILK
Meat and beans
Tofu
Vegetables
Fruits
CEREAL
OATMEAL
It's a fact!
Nutrition (noo TRISH uhn) is the science that deals with food and how the body uses it.
To view the food guides of different countries, turn to page 32 for a list of Web sites.

Grains

Grains are the seeds of grasses called cereals. Any food made from corn, wheat, rice, oats, or other cereal grain is part of the grains group. Grains are rich in carbohydrates (KAHR boh HY drayts). These nutrients give the body energy. Grains often make up the largest part of your diet.

Flour is made by grinding grains into a fine powder. Flour is used to make many foods, such as bread, pasta, and cookies.

Rice is the kernel of the rice plant.

Bobby's Test Kitchen

Bread is a mixture of flour and water that is baked in the oven. Many breads are made with whole grains.

It's a fact!

Scientists believe people in the Middle East started to grow grain plants for use as food more than 10,000 years ago!

Most **pasta** is made from wheat. It must be cooked in boiling water to make it soft.

Some **breakfast cereals** are made with whole grains. These are the healthiest choice.

Whole grains contain the whole grain kernel (seed). At least half of the grains you eat should be whole grains.

Vegetables

Vegetables are foods that come from plants. They are important sources of vitamins and minerals. These nutrients help keep the body healthy. Vegetables can be eaten raw or cooked. Try to eat vegetables of every color!

Dark green vegetables are a good source of many vitamins and minerals. You can steam many of these vegetables or eat them raw in a salad.

Carrots are the **roots** of the carrot plant. They have lots of vitamins.

It's a fact!

Dried beans and peas are part of the vegetable group. They're also part of the meat and beans group.

Spinach **leaves** are rich in vitamins and minerals.

Broccoli is the **flower** of the broccoli plant. It is rich in protein, minerals, and vitamins A and C.

Potatoes form underground on the **stems** of the potato plant.

Peas are the **seeds** of the pea plant. The peas are hidden inside the pod.

Fruits

Eat an **apple** or other piece of fruit as a healthy snack.

Fruits are part of flowering plants. They are important sources of many vitamins that help keep the body healthy. Eat them whole, cut them up, or toss them in the blender to make a smoothie!

Fruits and vegetables of different colors have different nutrients. Usually, the darker the color of the fruit or vegetable, the more nutrients it contains.

A medium orange is a **serving** of fruit.

Choose **dried fruits** that have no added sugar.

Cantaloupes and other melons taste sweet and juicy. They are good sources of vitamins A and C.

Drink small amounts of **fruit juice**.

A fruit holds the seeds of a plant. Seeds are the part of the plant that makes new plants.

Grapes come in many colors, from green to yellow, pink, red, dark blue, and black.

Bananas are rich in nutrients called carbohydrates. They also have minerals and vitamins A and C.

It's a fact!

Kiwi fruit is a berry that is rich in vitamin C. Just two kiwi fruits provide 240 percent of the vitamin C that you need for one day!

Where is the wheat growing?

Summer harvest

It's a lovely summer day and this farmer is harvesting grains, fruits, and vegetables.

Words you know

Here are some words that you learned earlier. Say them out loud, then try to find the things in the picture.

fruits grains leaves
stem vegetables melon

How many apples are growing on the tree?

Which items could you mix together to make a salad?

What colors are the bell peppers?

Which plants taste sweet?

What is the farmer picking?

Meat and beans

The meat and beans group includes beef, poultry (chicken and turkey), pork, and fish. It also includes dry beans and peas, tofu, eggs, nuts, and seeds. These foods have lots of protein. Protein is one of the main building materials of the body. Vegetarians get their protein from beans, grains, and vegetables.

Broiled, grilled, or baked **chicke[n]** is better for you than frie[d] chicken.

Lentils are part of the pea family. Lentil salad is a healthy lunch or dinner choice.

Some kinds of **fish** contain oils th[at] help keep your heart healthy. Nut[s] and seeds contain these oils, too.

It's a fact!

Peanuts are not actually nuts. They belong to a group called legumes. Legumes are plants with pods or shells.

Tofu is made from soybeans. It is low in fat and can be added to many dishes for protein.

Beef is a red meat that comes from adult cows. Extra-lean red meat is healthiest.

Dry beans must be soaked or boiled before eating. Try beans and rice for a tasty, nutritious meal.

For a healthy snack, try half a **peanut butter** and honey sandwich.

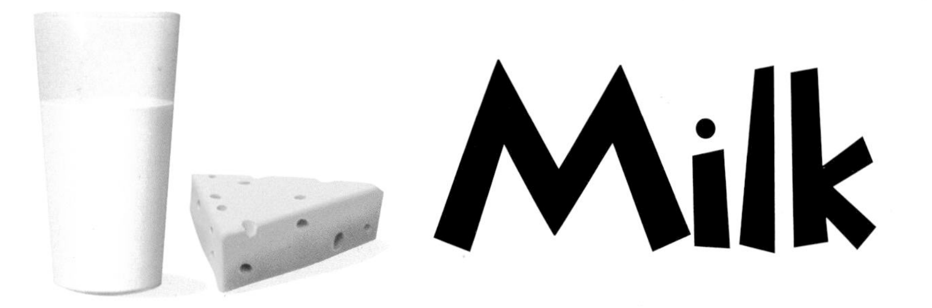

Milk

The milk group includes any foods made with milk. Calcium is a nutrient in milk that helps make your bones strong. Be sure to include low-fat or fat-free milk products in your diet.

Drinking a glass of **skim milk** is an easy way to eat from the milk group.

Cheese is one of the most important foods throughout the world. In factories, large machines stir milk to make the cheese.

Try unsweetened **yogurt** with fresh fruit and granola for a healthy breakfast.
yogurt
Yogurt
YOGURT
Cottage cheese and fresh pineapple make a healthy snack.
COTTAGE CHEESE
COTTAGE CHEESE
There are many kinds of **cheese.** Each has its own look and taste.
Milk
Milk
It's a fact!
Cows provide most of the milk used in many countries. But in some parts of the world, people drink milk from camels, goats, llamas, reindeer, sheep, and water buffalo.

Fats

Fats are not a food group, but we need small amounts of them every day. Fats give the body energy. Some fats are healthy, such as those from olives, nuts, or some fish. Others we should eat in small amounts, such as those from red meat and milk products.

Canned and packaged foods have a label that lists how much fat the food contains, along with other information.

Salmon is a kind of fish that has healthy fats.

It's a fact!

Olives are the fruit of the olive tree. These trees grow in warm regions of the world.

Olive oil is high in **unsaturated fat.** This is a healthy kind of fat.

Avocados are the fruits of the avocado tree. They are rich in vitamins, minerals, and healthy fats.

Butter is high in **saturated fat.** Too much of this kind of fat is bad for the heart.

Eating healthy

The amount of food you need to eat depends on many things, such as your age and how active you are. If you eat too much food, you can become overweight. If you don't eat enough food, you may develop other health problems. Work with a trusted adult to find the right food program for you.

Grains and vegetable should make up the biggest part of your meal.

United States First Lady Michelle Obama and students harvest vegetables from the White House garden. Michelle Obama planted the garden to help teach people about healthy eating.

Most of your meat and poultry choices should be **lean** (with little fat).

Baked or boiled foods are better for you than fried foods.

Eat **vegetables and fruits** for a healthy snack.

It's a fact!

Different countries have their own food guides. The guides are based on their food supply, customs, and the needs of their people.

Living healthy

Eating healthy foods helps the body fight off illness. It also helps the body get well when you are sick. But you must also keep an active mind and body to stay healthy!

1 Choosing the right kinds of foods gives the body energy.

2 **Exercise** helps keep the body healthy.

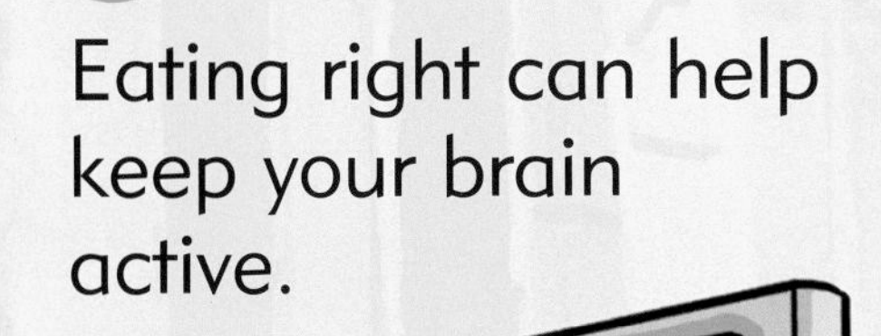

Eating right can help keep your brain active.

The body needs lots of **water** every day.

A good night's **sleep** helps restore the mind and body.

Limiting foods that are high in sugar can help protect your teeth.

It's a fact!

Some breakfast cereals sold in the United States are more than half sugar by weight. Too much sugar can lead to weight gain and other health problems.

How many milk products do you see?

Make it a good morning!

A good breakfast gives you the energy you need to have a great day! Choose healthy foods from the different food groups. A well-rounded meal will give you many of the nutrients your body needs.

How many people are eating fruits?

To which food group do eggs belong?

What is the girl eating?

Words you know

Here are some words that you learned earlier. Say them out loud, then try to find the things in the picture.

protein **fruit** **bread**

water **cottage cheese**

Which food group is missing?

How many people are eating grains?

Did you know?

Milk has almost all the main nutrients people need. It has water, carbohydrates, fats, proteins, vitamins, and minerals.

Wheat covers more of Earth's surface than any other food crop.

Sandwiches were named after the Earl of Sandwich, an English nobleman who lived in the 1700's. Legend has it that while playing cards, the Earl ordered a servant to bring him two slices of bread with a piece of roast meat between them.

Spanish explorers in South America first brought potatoes back to Europe around 1570. Soon after, potatoes spread to other parts of the world.

When ice cream is made, air bubbles are whipped into a milk mixture. If air were not added, ice cream would be as hard as ice cubes.

Quinoa *(KEE noh ah or KEEN wah)*, a whole grain, has been called the "mother grain" because of its importance to the ancient Inca of South America.

Puzzles

Close-up!

We've zoomed in on pictures of different foods. Can you guess what is in each picture?

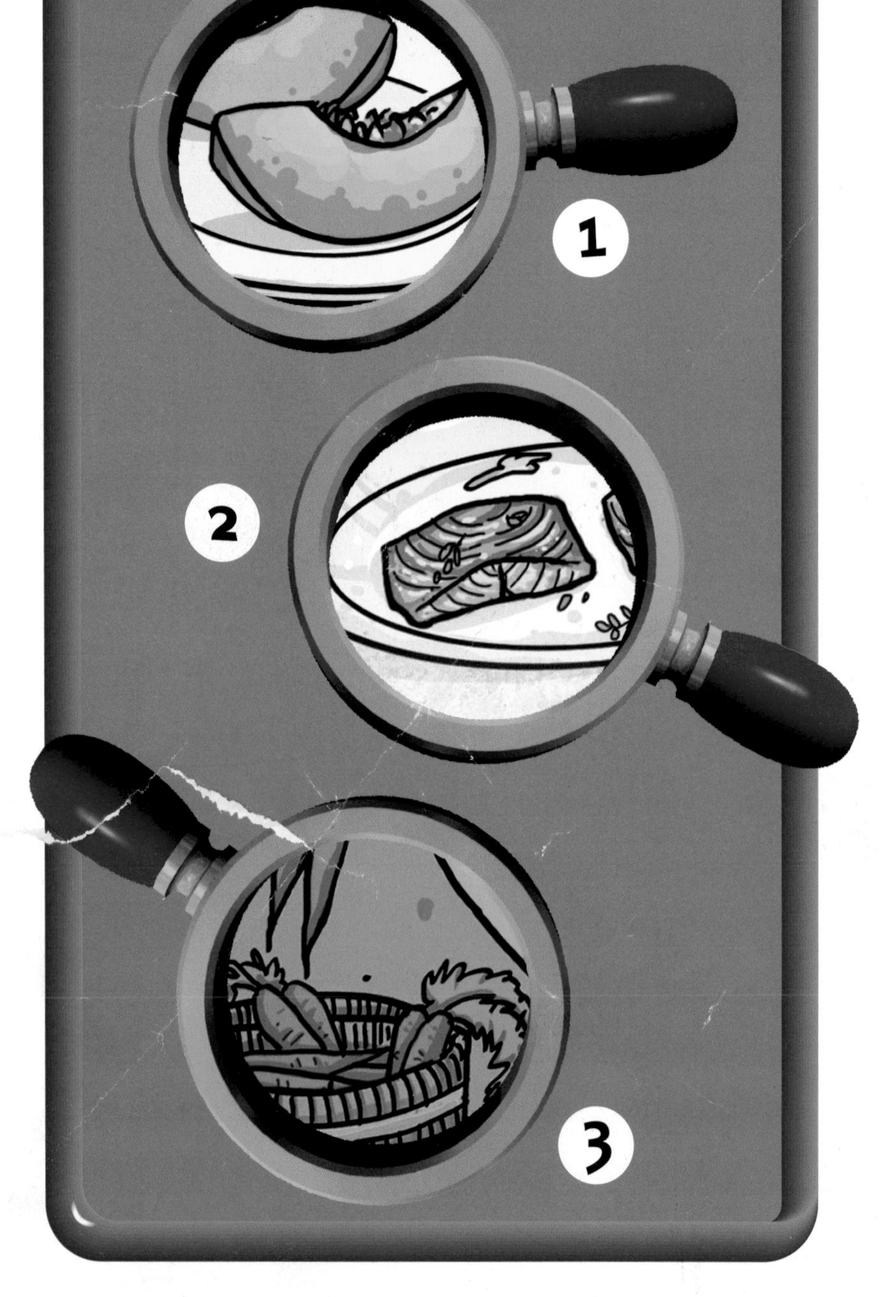

Answers on page 32.

Word jumble!

We've taken words from the book and mixed up the letters. Can you unscramble the letters to identify the words?

1. sraing
2. opotat
3. rawte
4. sneab
5. sechee
6. truifs

Match up!

Match each word on the left with the food group it belongs in.

1. turkey slices
2. spinach
3. wheat pasta
4. cottage cheese
5. bananas

- Grains
- Milk
- Fruits
- Meat and beans
- Vegetables

Answers on page 32.

True or false

Can you figure out which of these statements are true? Turn to the page numbers given to help you find the answers.

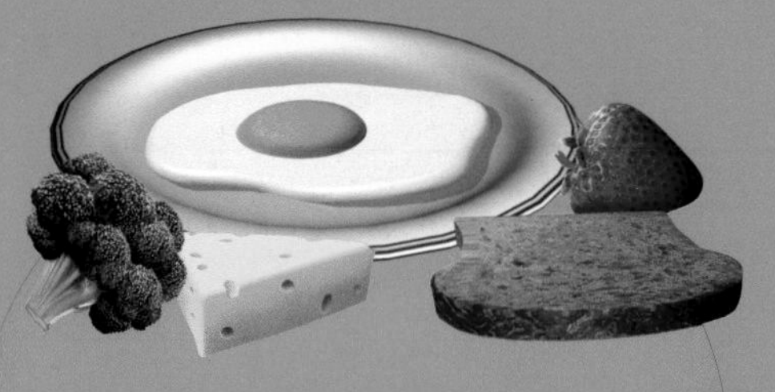

1

There are 7 main food groups.
Go to page 4.

2

Kiwi fruit is rich in vitamin C.
Go to page 11.

3

Milk products should make up the largest part of your diet.
Go to page 6.

4

Peanuts are not actually nuts.
Go to page 15.

5

Tofu is part of the meat and beans group.
Go to page 15.

Answers on page 32.

Find out more

Books

Eating Well by Liz Gogerly (Crabtree, 2009)
This story follows Ethan and James, two boys who learn about the importance of a proper diet.

Grover's Guide to Good Eating by Naomi Kleinberg (Random House, 2007)
Head waiter Grover (from Sesame Street) and his assistant Elmo welcome readers to the Good Eats Cafe, where they serve up tasty tidbits of information about healthy eating.

My Food Pyramid by Alisha Niehaus (DK Publishing, 2007)
This book uses the USDA Food Pyramid as a guideline to teach about healthy eating and living.

The New Food Guide Pyramid by Emily K. Green (Bellwether Media, 2007). Seven volumes: *Fruits; Grains; Meat and Beans; Healthy Eating; Milk, Yogurt, and Cheese; Oils; Vegetables.* Learn about the health benefits of healthy eating.

Websites

Ear Twiggles Fun in the Kitchen
http://www.eartwiggles.com/cookingwithchildren.html
A family website that suggests ways to give kids hands-on experience in preparing healthy foods.

My Plate Kids' Place
http://www.choosemyplate.gov/kids/index.html
Play games, watch videos, and more to learn all about healthy living and eating.

Nutrition Explorations
http://www.nutritionexplorations.org/kids/main.asp
Learn about building a healthy body by playing games, coloring pages, following recipes, and entering a contest.

Staying Healthy
http://kidshealth.org/kid/stay_healthy/
Find out the basics of nutrition, how to prepare healthy foods, and ways to keep fit.

Answers

Puzzles

from pages 28 and 29

Close-up!

1. cantaloupe 2. salmon 3. carrots

Word jumble!

1. grains 2. potato 3. water
4. beans 5. cheese 6. fruits

Match up!

1. meat and beans 2. vegetables
3. grains 4. milk 5. fruits

True or false

from page 30

1. false 2. true 3. false
4. true 5. true

Index

Resources for parents and educators

Child Care: Nutrition (India) http://india.gov.in/citizen/health/nutrition.php

Dietary Guidelines for All Australians http://www.nhmrc.gov.au/publications/synopses/dietsyn.htm

Eating for Healthy Children Aged 2 to 12 (New Zealand)
http://www.healthed.govt.nz/resources/eatingforhealthychildrenaged2to12t.aspx

Eatwell (United Kingdom) http://www.eatwell.gov.uk/

Food and Nutrition: Canada's Food Guide, Advice for Different Ages and Stages
http://www.hc-sc.gc.ca/fn-an/index-eng.php

Food Composition Table for Pakistan (Revised 2001) http://www.aiou.edu.pk/FoodSite/FCTViewOnLine.html

Healthy Eating for Children (South Africa)
http://5-a-day.co.za/images/Healthy%20Eating%20for%20Children.pdf

Philippines National Dietary Guidelines for the Philippines
http://www.afic.org/National%20Dietary%20Guidelines%20for%20the%20Philippines.htm